A Concise
Introduction
to UNIX

ALSO AVAILABLE

A Concise Introduction to UNIX

by
Noel Kantaris

**BERNARD BABANI (publishing) LTD
THE GRAMPIANS
SHEPHERDS BUSH ROAD
LONDON W6 7NF
ENGLAND**

PLEASE NOTE

Although every care has been taken with the production of this book to ensure that any projects, designs, modifications and/or programs etc. contained herewith, operate in a correct and safe manner and also that any components specified are normally available in Great Britain, the Publishers and Author do not accept responsibility in any way for the failure, including fault in design, of any project, design, modification or program to work correctly or to cause damage to any other equipment that it may be connected to or used in conjunction with, or in respect of any other damage or injury that may be so caused, nor do the Publishers accept responsibility in any way for the failure to obtain specified components.

Notice is also given that if equipment that is still under warranty is modified in any way or used or connected with home-built equipment then that warranty may be void.

© 1988 BERNARD BABANI (publishing) LTD

First Published — November 1988

British Library Cataloguing in Publication Data:
Kantaris, Noel
   A concise introduction to UNIX.
   1. Computer systems. Operating Systems: UNIX
   I. Title
   005.4'3

ISBN 0 85934 204 2

Typeset direct from disk by Commercial Colour Press, London E7.
Printed and Bound in Great Britain by Cox & Wyman Ltd, Reading

ABOUT THE BOOK

To help the beginner, this concise introduction to UNIX and its many 'look-alike' operating environments, has been structured on the basis of "what you need to know first, appears first". However, the structure of the book is such that you don't have to start at the beginning and go right through to the end. The more experienced user can start from any section, as they have been designed to be self contained.

This book does not seek to replace the documentation you receive with the UNIX operating system; its purpose is to explain and supplement it. However, the guide was written with the non-expert, busy person in mind. One doesn't need to read several hundred pages on UNIX to find out almost all there is to know about the operating system, when 50 pages can do the same thing quite adequately!

With the help of this small book, it is hoped that you will be able to get the most out of your computer in terms of efficiency and productivity, and that you will be able to do it in the shortest, most effective and informative way.

ABOUT THE AUTHOR

Graduated in Electrical Engineering at Bristol University and after spending three years in the Electronics Industry in London, took up a Tutorship in Physics at the University of Queensland. Research interests in Ionospheric Physics, lead to the degrees of M.E. in Electronics and Ph.D. in Physics. On return to the UK, he took up a Post-Doctoral Research Fellowship in Radio Physics at the University of Leicester, and in 1973 a Senior Lectureship in Engineering at The Camborne School of Mines, Cornwall, where since 1978 he has also assumed the responsibility of Head of Computing.

ACKNOWLEDGEMENTS

I would like to thank colleagues at the Camborne School of Mines for the helpful tips and suggestions which assisted me in the writing of this book.

TRADEMARKS

CONTENTS

INTRODUCTION

The UNIX operating system was first developed in the early 1970s at AT&T's Bell Laboratories in the United States. Since then more than twenty variants of the original have appeared as the concept has gained popularity. Efforts have been made to agree on a standard that will run on anything from a mainframe to a PC, regardless of the manufacturer of the hardware. The American National Standards Institute (ANSI) has drawn up specifications for a look-alike UNIX operating system to be known by the name of POSIX and lately, IBM, DEC, HP and others, have formed the Open Systems Foundation (OSF), in an attempt to develop the definitive standard for UNIX, based on IBM's own version of the system, called AIX.

It is more likely than not, that in the next year or so, one unified standard will emerge which will make this operating system even more popular than it is at present. UNIX's popularity rests on the fact that it already runs on endless different makes of computers. It has become the de facto standard for multi-user applications. Just as DOS has become the standard operating system for single-user, single-task applications, and OS/2 is gaining ground as the only possible standard for single-user multi-tasking operations, UNIX is already the standard for multi-user applications. Writing a program in a portable language, such as C (the language UNIX itself is written in), Cobol or Fortran 77 and then being able to run these programs on any computer running UNIX without any change whatsoever is very attractive indeed. DOS has already achieved this for the single-user, single-task applications.

Already the UNIX and DOS operating systems are drawing closer and closer in the way they present themselves and feel to the user and attempts are being made to unify them. If you have used DOS (you might call it PC-DOS or MS-DOS), then you already know quite a lot about UNIX. At first sight, some UNIX commands might appear difficult to understand particularly if your first encounter with them is through the operating manuals which were designed, after all, as reference and not as learning manuals. You will soon, however, get used to UNIX's commands, whether you have experience of DOS or not, as there is an underlying simplicity to the system's commands which when understood, will make your task a lot easier.

1

This book seeks to exploit this inherent simplicity of the UNIX operating system by presenting, with simple examples, the commands you need to know, when you need to know them. At the same time, the book has been written in such a way as to also act as a reference guide, long after you have mastered most of the operating commands of standard UNIX.

Logging in

As a user of a machine running the UNIX operating system you would expect to be able to use a terminal to perform various operations, such as entering a program into the computer, saving it on disc, executing it and obtaining an output on the VDU (Visual Display Unit) or the printer. However, before you can do anything at all, you must log in which is a method of identifying yourself to the system. In order to log in, you need to have a 'username' and a 'password', which are normally obtainable from the manager of your computer installation.

Thus, if everything is running smoothly, when you approach a terminal, the word

Login:

should be in display. If this is not the case, it could mean that the previous user has forgot to log off from the system, in which case typing 'Ctrl D' (press the Ctrl key and while holding it down press the letter D), should log off the previous user and restore the system. Be careful when you press 'Ctrl D' that you don't press 'Ctrl S' instead (which stops scrolling of information on the screen) as anything typed after it appears as having no effect on the system. If you type 'Ctrl S', then follow it by 'Ctrl Q' which resumes scrolling, thus allowing the system to respond to further commands.

In reply to 'login' you should type in your 'username' and press the Return key. Remember to use lower case letters when typing your 'username', as UNIX prefers to work with lower case, and don't include any spaces. If all is well, and a password has been allocated to you, then you will get the response

Password:

after which you type in your password and again press the Return key.

Remember that the computer does not respond to your input until you press the Return key. Also, what you type in as your password is not echoed on the VDU as it is supposed to be known to you only. Again, if all is well you will perhaps get a message from the computer manager, followed by the

$

prompt. The '$' prompt means that you can start your session with the computer, entering programs or commands. It is quite possible that your system might have a different prompt to the one shown above, as this largely depends on which 'shell' your system is currently running.

Everything done under the UNIX operating system is done through separate small programs, such as **login** which is a special program that interacts with the user and is always the first one to be run by the operating system. The particular shell used in your system (there are several different ones available, some of which are named after their originators), is also a program that is run by UNIX immediately after the **login** program. This program reads the keyboard and interprets what you type in. If you type a command with an argument (an option given with a command), the shell makes sure that the commands are carried out, by running the appropriate small program, and passing to it the arguments you provided. UNIX is simply the supervisor under which all these command programs are running.

Changing a Password

UNIX allows you to change you password with the use of a special program called **passwd.** The program can be invoked by first logging in, typing your current password and then typing the command

passwd

at which stage the computer will ask you to retype your current password to make sure your are not somebody else trying to change the previous user's password who forgot to log off the system. Having satisfied the system that you are who you say you are, the program then asks you for the new password. Since what you type is not echoed on the screen, the system asks you to verify the newly chosen password by retyping it. If both entries are the same, the system accepts your new password.

3

Needless to say that you must be very careful when changing your password. If you type something in twice with the same mistake, unbeknown to you, then you will have problems later. It is best to approach your computer manager before attempting to change your password and let him/her do it for you. After all it is a good idea to have someone else in authority know your password in case you forget it one day, which you are bound to do!

DIRECTORIES & FILES

Many UNIX commands deal with file manipulation. A file is an area on disc containing a program or data. If you were using a normal filing system, then organizing the files you keep is relatively straight forward. The usual method would be to keep similar file applications on the same drawer of a filing cabinet, so that one such drawer might contain files on letters, another on programs, another on lists of clients, and so on.

The same thing can be emulated on the hard disc of a computer system with UNIX keeping track of all such files by allocating space on separate parts of the disc, called a directory, to store similar subject files. In addition, the system keeps such information as the name of each file, its size, the date it was last amended, and so on. Users could, of course, keep all their files on the one directory allocated to them, but as the number of such files increase and the amount of information you can store increases, unless some sort of file organization was imposed on the system, one could easily spend all of their time trying to find an important file.

UNIX helps us to organize our files on disc by providing a system of directories and sub-directories. The key to the system is the 'root' directory, indicated by the slash sign (/), which is the main directory under which a number of sub-directories exist. In turn, each sub-directory can have its own sub-directories, as shown below.

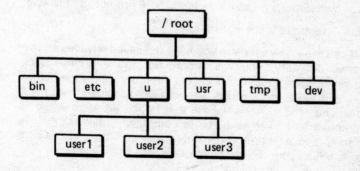

5

The root directory is shown here with six sub-directories under it, while one of these (the u sub-directory) is shown with its own three sub-directories below it.

The u sub-directory is of particular interest to users, as it is through this *path* that their own 'home' directory is connected to the root directory. The root directory normally contains only the System routines and start up files, together with information on its sub-directories, a kind of an index drawer to an office filing system. The other sub-directories to the root directory contain files which help to administer the system, such as command and shell files, language compilers, library routines, device drivers, etc.

Files in different sub-directories can have the same name because UNIX can be told which is which via a system of **path** names. For example, a file in the **user1** sub-directory could have the same name, say **program.for**, as one in the **user2** sub-directory. Nevertheless, we can instruct UNIX to fetch the file in the **user1** sub-directory by giving its path name which is:

/u/user1/program.for

whereas that of the file in the **user2** sub-directory is:

/u/user2/program.for

The list command
To see what files are held in your 'home' directory, you must have logged in to the system—which automatically puts you in your own directory—and type **ls** at the $ prompt, as follows:

$ ls   (and press the Return key)

If you are a new user and you have not saved any files on your 'home' directory, you will simply get the $ prompt back. However, there are two files in your directory, called the '.' (dot) and '..' (double dot), which are normally not listed with the ls command. The '.' file is the file that **ls** first accesses when no arguments are given with the **ls** command, while the '..' file refers to one level up the UNIX directory structure, in this case /**u**, in which your 'home' directory is listed as an entry.

To see these files, type **ls -al** which is the list command with two arguments, normally referred to as 'qualifiers'; a stands for 'all files', while l stands for 'long listing format'. Qualifiers are traditionally indicated by the '-' sign following the command. Thus, on typing

ls −al

in your 'home' directory, before saving any other files, the following listing is displayed:

```
drwxr-xr-x   3   206   230   160   07 Jun 11.15   .
drwxr-xr-x   2   206   230   112   07 Jun 11.15   ..
```

where the preceding 'd' tells us that what is listed are directories, 'rwxr-xr-x' tells us who has file access permission according to the following list:

first **rwx** refers to the 'owner'
second **rwx** refers to the 'group'
third **rwx** refers to 'all other' users, with
r = permission to read directory contents,
w = permission to write to directory, and
x = permission to access directory entries, with
− in place of r, w, or x meaning 'no permission'.

the numbers 3 and 2, following the permissions string, refers to the number of 'links' to these directories whose user number, group number, length in number of characters, date and time of creation follow in order of appearance, as shown. Finally, '.' indicates the file that ls first accesses, and '..' indicates the file that refers to one level up the UNIX directory structure.

Managing sub-directories

It is often convenient to create a sub-directory to your 'home' directory in which to keep groups of similar files, say documents, which you wish to keep separate from those in the 'home' directory which might contain program files. UNIX provides three special commands for the creation and management of sub-directories. These are:

Command	Meaning	Example
mkdir	Make sub-directory	$ mkdir docs
cd	Change directory	$ cd docs
rmdir	Remove directory	$ rmdir docs

7

Before a sub-directory can be used, it must exist. If it does not, you can make it with the **mkdir** command.

To make the sub-directory called **docs**, so that you could transfer to it or save into it all your document files, type the following command

```
$ mkdir docs
$
```

which makes the **docs** sub-directory to your home directory and waits for further commands. Note that the full path from the root (/) directory was not given after the **mkdir** command, which if you refer back to the directory diagram should have been

```
$ mkdir /u/user1/docs
```

which specifies first the root directory with the use of the slash (/) and then the sub-directories **u/user1/docs**. Instead, we created sub-directory **docs** relative to the currently logged directory (**user1**). Now typing

```
$ cd docs
```

at the prompt, changes the current directory to that of **docs**. If you are not sure where you are in the directory structure, simply type the **pwd** command which stands for 'present working directory', as follows:

```
$ pwd
```

which, if you are in the **docs** sub-directory, should evoke the response

```
$ /u/user1/docs
```

Files can be copied or moved from one directory to another very easily with the help of certain commands. But before we go any further, it would be a good idea to learn how to create a file with the help of the **ed** line editor, so that we can introduce these and other commands to files created by you, the user. A summary of UNIX's commands are listed, for quick reference, in the last section of this book.

8

THE ED LINE EDITOR

UNIX provides us with a simple line editor, called **ed**, and you should become familiar with its use. In general, **ed** allows the creation and editing of ASCII files. These are text files which when sent to the screen or printer are interpreted as text. Ed can also be used to create source code files for various programming languages, such as Fortran or C, in which case, remember to give the file the appropriate extension. For the two languages mentioned above, these will be **.for** and **.c**, respectively.

To invoke **ed**, simply type its name and follow it by the name of the file you want to create or edit, as follows:

$ ed test.txt

which causes ed to look for the fictitious file **test.txt** on the disc in the logged directory. The line editor **ed** normally resides in a directory other than the one you are logged into currently.

If the file **test.txt** does not exist, then ed responds with

? test.txt

The query (?) is **ed**'s response to instructions it does not expect—in this case because the file does not exist—and waits for further commands. If the file already exists, then **ed** loads the file into RAM and responds with a number indicating the file's size in bytes, for example

321

Let us now create a text file, called **test.txt**, which we will use to demonstrate the power of **ed**. To start, type at the prompt the command

$ ed test.txt

which should cause **ed** to respond with

? test.txt

if that file does not exist on your logged directory. If it does exist and you do not want to spoil its contents, then type **q** (for quit) and press the Return key.

The Append Command:
To append lines of text, use the command **a** (for append). In the case of a new file, as no lines of text exist in the file, type **a** and then type in the short text given below, pressing the Return key at the end of each line.

a
first line of text
second line of text
third line of text
fourth line of text

The contents between **a** and . (dot), are appended to the the empty file. As ed does not give any prompt at all, the text given above is exactly what you see on the screen. The dot ends the appending mode and also marks the last line of text (in this case line 4), as the *current line*. The current line is also known as the *dot* line, but still refers to the last line of text to be entered, changed or listed. To find out which line is the current (or dot) line, type 'n' which will display its number. Typing '.', will display the contents of the current line, while '$ = ' displays the number of the very last line in the file.

The List Command:
To see what text is in the file, type **l** (for list), as follows:

l
fourth line of text

   The line listed by **ed** is the current line (the last line of text appended previously).
   To list specific lines, use the **l** command with line numbers. For example,

1,3l

will list lines from 1 to 3 inclusive, while

2,$l

will list lines from 2 to the end of file, as the $ symbol is taken to mean 'end of file'.

Note the command syntax which is: 'From start number to end number list'. There must be no comma between the second line number and the command letter. Also note that listing lines causes the 'current line' to be changed to the last listed line.

The Write Command:

Created text can be saved to disc by writing it to file, using the w command. Thus, typing

w

will cause the above two lines of text to be written to the test.txt file.

From that point on, you could quit ed by typing

q

Had the text not been written to file or edited in any way since the last write to file, ed will respond with

?

and replying by pressing q again, will quit the editor with consequent loss of information.

The Change Command:

To change a specific line of text, type its number, followed by c (for change), which first deletes from the buffer the contents of the line to be changed. If the line number is omitted then it is assumed that you intend to change the current line. In either case, this puts you in the change mode and anything you type will replace the intended line.

In our case, we want to change line 2 to

second line of text, edited

so, enter the change mode by typing

2c

and change the line appropriately by re-typing it and typing '.' (dot) to terminate the change mode.

The Insert Command on an Existing File:

To insert lines of text, use the command **i** (for insert). However, be warned. Using **i** by its own will insert the new line *before* the current line. To insert lines at any other point, give the line number before the command.

In our case, we would like to insert one additional line in between the first two lines. To do this, type

2i
in between line
.

Again, insertion mode is terminated by typing a dot. If we now list the first three lines of the file, we get:

1,3l
first line of text
in between line
second line of text, edited

Note that the last line to be inserted becomes the current line (in this case line 2) which was the case prior to issuing the list command, after which line 3 becomes the current line as it is the last line to be listed.

The Delete Command:

To delete unwanted lines of text, use the **d** command (for delete). However, if you use the **d** command without any number associated with it, you will delete the current line. Therefore, if you want to delete line 2, say, type

2d

or if you want to delete a group of lines, type

13,15d

which is translated as 'lines 13 to 15 to be deleted'. If the range given is beyond the file-end, **ed** responds with its usual '?'.

The Move and Transcribe Commands:

To move or transcribe (copy) text, use the **m** or **t** commands (for move or transcribe). These commands must be preceded by numbers, as follows:

13,15m8
13,15m$

which is interpreted as 'lines 13 to 15 to be moved to a position *after* line 8', and 'lines 13 to 15 to be moved to the end of the file', respectively. If the range given is beyond the file-end, ed responds with its usual '?'.

Similarly, the **t** command will transcribe a block and insert it *after* the given line. To move or transcribe a single line, precede the command with only one number. If the command letter is given without a leading line number, ed assumes you want to operate on the current line.

The Search Command:

To search for the occurrence of a word or a specified number of characters in a file you have created using **ed**, use the search command. Just as in the list and delete commands, a line range could be specified, followed by the string to be searched for in slashes. The command

/edited/

will start a search for 'edited' from the current line to the end of the file, and if it does not find a match, it will continue from the beginning of the file. Thus, each line of the file is searched forwards from the current line. When a match is found, the contents of the matched line are displayed. Typing 'n', will give its line number.

The search command finds only the first occurrence of the specified string. To continue the search for further occurrences of the same string, simply type

//

again, as **ed** remembers the last pattern used. Thus, typing

/ir/
first line of text
//
third line of text

causes **ed** to first find the string 'ir' in the word 'first' of line 1, then by typing //, it displays the second occurrence of the same string 'ir' in the word 'third' of line 3. However, pressing the Return key, displays the contents of the next numbered line in the file irrespective of search pattern.

The Substitute Command:

This command is similar to the search command, except that it requires the s command and a replacement string. Thus, typing

1,4s/edited/re-edited/

will cause the *first* occurrence of the word 'edited' within the specified line range of text, to be replaced by the word 're-edited'. Here, of course, it occurs once in line 2 of the text.

If you want to substitute *all* occurrences of the specified string by another within the given range, then use the **g** (for global) option, as follows:

1,4s/edited/re-edited/g

If only one line number is specified before the s command, only that line will be affected. Further, the command

s/re-//

will replace the word 're-' by nothing, effectively deleting it, provided the characters 're-' are to be found on the current line, otherwise ed will respond with '?'.

Similarly, the **&** option could be used to insert characters either before or after a specified string, depending on the position of the **&**. For example,

s/line/&d/
s/line/under&/

will replace the string 'line' with 'lined' in the first case, and 'line' with 'underline' in the second case.

Pattern matching:

There several characters used by **ed** in 'pattern matching', which allow the specification of patterns of characters to be used with either the search or substitute (**s**) command.

There are two special characters which can specify the position of a search pattern within a line. For example, the search pattern

/^third/

will find the next line that *starts* with the string which follows the carat (^). Thus, the carat forces the search for a pattern which occurs at the beginning of a line.

The second character we can use to specify a search pattern is the dollar ($) character. It forces the search for a pattern which occurs at the end of a line. Thus,

/edited$/

will look for the occurrence of the string 'edited' at the end of a line.

The carat and the dollar can be combined to specify both the beginning and the end of a line. For example,

/^first$/

will only match the string 'first' with a line containing *only* the specified string.

Finally, there are two special characters which are used as wildcard characters to specify a given pattern. Of these, the dot (.) is used to specify any single character within a string, while the asterisk (*) is used to specify any number of the preceding character. For example,

/l.ne/

will find all occurrences of 'lane', 'line' and 'lone', while

/g*/
/g.*/

means any number of the letter g, and any number of any characters following the letter g, respectively.

Exiting ed:
To end the current session and exit **ed** at any point, type

w

which writes to disc the contents of the file under the chosen filename, then type

q

to quit the editor.

If, on the other hand, you realised that too many mistakes were made during editing, you could use the **q** command to quit ed, but without first writing to disc with the **w** command. This will invoke the

?

response, to which you will have to reply by pressing **q** again.

The **ed** line editor supports a wealth of extra commands which were not discussed above. The commands presented are more than adequate for writing and editing all but the most difficult programs. If you intend to write extremely complicated programs which will require extensive editing, then it is best to use a full screen editor or your word processor, provided, of course, your word processor can export files in ASCII format.

MANAGING FILES

Let us now assume that your 'home' directory is **user1** and you have already saved some files in it, with names consisting of letters and digits not exceeding 14 characters in length. Further, let us assume that the names of these files are **prog1.for** and **prog2.for**, both being Fortran source code files, hence the **.for** extension to the filename which the Fortran compiler (not UNIX) requires. Other extensions commonly used by compilers, interpreters or users are:

.c   .bas   .dta   .doc   .tmp   .txt

which indicate 'C' source programs, 'Basic' programs, 'data' files, 'document' files, 'temporary' files and 'text' files, respectively.

On listing the directory now, the following list of files and associated information will be displayed:

```
-rw-------   1   206   230   255   05   Jun   11.15   prog1.for
-rw-------   1   206   230   198   05   Jun   11.15   prog2.for
```

where the preceding ' − ' indicates a file, and 'rwxrwxrwx' tells us who has file access permission according to the following list:

> first **rwx** refers to the 'owner'
> second **rwx** refers to the 'group'
> third **rwx** refers to 'all other' users, with
> r = permission to read file contents,
> w = permission to write to file, and
> x = permission to execute file, with
> − in place of r, w, or x meaning 'no permission'

Thus, in the above case, the owner of files **prog1.for** and **prog2.for** can read and write to these files, while members of the group and others are excluded.

Changing permissions
A user may change access permissions to any of his/her files by using the **chmod** (change mode) command and specifying the filename to be operated upon. The general form of the command is:

chmod mode filename

17

where mode is normally specified by using the symbolic form

[ugoa] [+ - =] [rwxstugo]

where the optional characters within the various square brackets have the following meaning:

[ugoa]

u	user (owner)
g	group
o	others
a	all

[+ - =]

+	add permissions
-	subtract permissions
=	replace permissions

[rwxstugo]

r	read
w	write
x	execute
s	set owner or group identity
t	save text
ugo	user/group/others—permission to be taken from present mode

An example will help to illustrate the above command. The first file listed earlier was as follows:

-rw------- 1 206 230 255 05 Jun 11.15 prog1.for

where the owner of the file could read and write to it, while group members and others could not. Let us assume now that we want to give permission of reading the file to both the group members and others. The **chmod** command we would have to issue would be:

chmod go + r prog1.for

and, on listing the file, we would get

-rw-r--r-- 1 206 230 255 05 Jun 11.15 prog1.for

indicating that the symbolic expression 'go + r' had the effect of adding read permission to members of the group and others.

Copying and moving files

Let us assume that your 'home' directory is **user1** and that you have files **letter1.txt**, **letter2.txt**, **prog1.for** and **prog2.for** saved in it.

You can copy a file into another file by the use of the cp (for copy) command, as follows:

$ cp letter1.txt letter3.txt

which will copy the contents of file **letter1.txt** into file **letter3.txt**, thus making an identical copy of the original file. The command can be interpreted as:

copy *from* filename1 *to* filename2

After execution of the command, two identical files are to be found on the user's directory. However, be careful when using the copy command because, if any information had existed in the file you are copying to, in this case **letter3.txt**, that information would be lost.

One quick way of verifying that both files are the same, is to list your directory. The two files in question should have the same length. However, two files having the same length is not enough guarantee that the files are identical, unless you have just happened to use the copy command to create one of them. To find out whether two files are identical, then use the **diff** command on the two files, as follows:

$ diff letter1.txt letter3.txt
$

which will return the $ prompt, if the two files are identical.

Files can be copied from your 'home' directory to an already existing sub-directory, say **docs** (which was created with the use of the **mkdir** command), as follows:

$ cp letter1.txt docs

which copies the file **letter1.txt** to sub-directory **docs**, giving it the same name as its current name. The format of the command would be slightly different had we changed our logged directory to that of **docs** with the command

$ cd docs

in which case we would have had to use

$ cp ../letter1.txt .

which is interpreted as 'copy **letter.txt** from the parent directory (identified by ../) to the current directory (identified by .)'.

The contents of a file can be moved into another file with the use of the **mv** (for move) command, as follows:

$ mv letter1.txt letter4.txt

which essentially renames file **letter1.txt** to **letter4.txt** with the results that the original filename does not exist any more.

Using wildcard characters

To move all files from the currently logged 'home' directory to, say, the **docs** sub-directory, we can type

$ mv * docs

Note the most useful character in UNIX, namely '*' meaning 'all filenames with all extensions'. The '*' is known as the wildcard character which stands for 'all'.

However, if we needed to move a set of files, say all those files with the extension **.txt**, from the currently logged 'home' directory to the **docs** sub-directory, we would type

$ mv *.txt docs

which means 'move *from* the current directory *all* files with extension **.txt** *to* the docs sub-directory'.

The wildcard character '*' can also be used as part of the filename. For example,

$ ls letter*.txt

will list all files with the extension **txt** which start with the word **letter**.

A more precise wildcard is the query character '?' which can be substituted for a single character in a filename.

For example, assuming that there are several consecutively numbered files on your 'home' directory with filenames **prog1.for** to **prog2.for**, typing

$ ls prog?.for

will list all files with the extension **.for**, from **prog1** to **prog9**, but not those within the range **prog10** to **prog999**. On the other hand, using two consecutive query characters in the filename, such as

$ ls prog??.for

will list all files with the extension **.for**, from **prog10** to **prog99**, but exclude those within the range **prog100** to **prog999**.

Removing files and directories
Should you want to delete files from your currently logged directory, use the **rm** (for remove) command, as follows:

$ rm letter*.txt

which will remove all files with the extension **txt** which start with the word **letter**.

Should you be dissatisfied with the name of a directory, you could rename it (we will discuss this later), but for the time being we will follow a longer route so as to show how certain other commands can be used. We will choose to make another directory giving it our preferred name, move to it all files from the unwanted directory, and then remove the unwanted directory from its parent directory, using the **rmdir** command, as follows:

$ rmdir docs

while logged on the 'home' directory. This procedure is essential because directories can not be removed unless they are empty.

As an example of the above procedure, let as assume that we have created, as discussed previously, a sub-directory to the **user1** 'home' directory, called **docs** which contains several files. Now create a new sub-directory to the **user1** directory, called **documents** by typing

$ mkdir documents

Then change directories to the newly created sub-directory **documents**, as follows:

```
$ cd documents
```

and move all files from **docs** to **documents**, by typing

```
$ mv ../docs/* .
```

which means 'move all files (*) *from* the sub-directory **docs** which is listed on the parent directory of the logged (**../docs/**) sub-directory *to* the logged (.) sub-directory'.

Verify that your command has been executed by listing the contents of both **documents** and **docs** sub-directories. When you are satisfied that all is well, change directory to the 'home' directory by typing

```
$ cd ..
```

and remove the unwanted **docs** sub-directory by typing

```
$ rmdir docs
```

We shall now do the same thing, but this time moving all files from sub-directory **documents** to **docs**, but without moving from the 'home' directory. To do this, type

```
$ mkdir docs
$ mv ./documents/* ./docs
$ rmdir documents
```

which first makes a sub-directory docs to the 'home' directory, then moves *all* (*) files from sub-directory **documents** to sub-directory **docs**, and finally removes sub-directory **documents**.

We could shorten the above procedure even further by using the command

```
$ mv documents docs
```

which simply *renames* the sub-directory **documents** to **docs**.

As you can see, there is a shorter way for achieving our intended goal, but don't dismiss the longer route, as it teaches you more about certain commands.

INDIRECTION COMMANDS

Most UNIX commands take their input from the keyboard, which is known as the 'standard input device'. Likewise, most commands send their output to the VDU screen, which is known as the 'standard output device'. However, a feature of the shell is 'indirection' which allows both input and output to be taken from or sent to a specified device, such as a file for input and output, or a printer for output.

Output from a command can be sent to a file by specifying this with the character '>', followed by the filename. For example, typing

$ echo Hi, there! > salute

sends the greeting 'Hi, there!' to the file called **salute**. Normally, the command **echo**, echoes what follows it, plus a line feed, to the VDU screen (the standard output device), but by including the indirection character > at the end of the command argument, it sends instead the argument to the specified file.

The fact that the command automatically adds a line feed at the end of its argument list, allows us to build up a file with several lines. For example, we can add another line to the contents of **salute**, by typing

$ echo How are you today? >> salute

which concatenates (adds) the present line to the end of the existing contents of **salute**, plus an additional line feed.

To see what is held in the file, type

$ cat salute

which should send the contents of the **salute** file to the VDU. The name of the command (**cat**) arises from the fact that it can 'concatenate' several files and send its output either to the VDU, a file or the printer.

Thus, typing

$ cat salute salute

should result in the double display of the contents of file **salute** on the VDU.

Similarly, indirection of input is achieved with the use of the < character, plus the name of the file from which input is to be obtained.

Pipes and filters

The shell program (an interface between the user and UNIX) allows the standard output of one command to be connected to the standard input of another. To illustrate the point, consider an example in which we would like to print the contents of, say, three separate files in order to check their content. One way of doing this is as follows:

$ cat file1 file2 file3 | print

which takes the standard output of the **cat** command, which is the VDU, and sends it through a pipe, indicated by the (|) character, to the printer queue. When commands are used in this manner, they are known as 'filters'.

As an example, let us consider the **more** filter command which allows us to view text files a page (23 lines) at a time—the user is prompted to press a key before the next page is displayed. As such, it can be combined with other commands to control scrolling of long ASCII files. For example,

$ cat file1 file2 file3 | more

or even used by itself (giving quicker response) as

$ more longfile

can help with the viewing of long text files.

If you are an AIX user, then substitute the command **pg**, which stands for 'paged', in place of **more** in the above examples.

Multiple command line

Sometimes it is convenient to issue multiple commands on one line before pressing the Return key to start execution of these commands. Up to now we have considered only one command per line which was executed the moment we pressed the Return key.

Had we required to follow this command by another one, we would have had to wait until the first was terminated before issuing any further commands. The shell allows us to combine several command per line, provided we separate them with a semicolon (;).

Let us assume that we have a file called **namelist** which contains the names of clients and that we wish to obtain a printout of the list in alphabetical order. Furthermore, let us assume that, for some reason or another, we would like to retain the unsorted original list. Normally, we would have to issue the following commands:

```
$ sort − d namelist > sorted
$ cat sorted
$ rm sorted
```

which causes each line to be executed before we can type the next line. We have included the − d qualified in the **sort** command which means 'in dictionary order'.

Using the facility of entering multiple commands on the same line, the above example would be written as:

```
$ sort − d namelist > sorted ; cat sorted ; rm sorted
```

which is all typed in one line, before pressing the Return key. The effect of the semicolon on the shell is to take each section separately and execute it, before proceeding to the next, as if we had typed each section on separate lines

Background execution

After issuing a command, the shell program waits for the execution of the command to terminate before returning the prompt to the screen. This means that, if you issued a command the execution of which is time consuming —such as sending a long concatenated file to the printer or using a sort on a large data file, you will have to wait until it is done. However, there is a way whereby such commands can be executed in the background while you edit another file, or do something else.

To order the shell to execute a command in the background, you must use the ampersand (&) character at the end of the command. For example,

```
$ sort − n long.dta > sorted.dta &
```

will carry out the command in the background because of the '&' sign appearing at the end. It is assumed that file **long.dta** holds numerical data, as the qualifier ' − n' sorts numbers by value and not by ASCII. Further, in order to avoid having the output from the **sort** command appear on the screen in the middle of whatever work we are then are doing, it has been sent to the **sorted.dta** file instead.

Multiple background commands

When multiple commands are issued on the same line and at the same time we would like to have them executed in background, then we must enclose these commands in brackets and type the ampersand (**&**) after the closing bracket.

We can illustrate this by taking the earlier example of our clients list, in which we required to obtain a printout of a sorted list, without retaining the sorted file.

Thus, typing

$ (sort − d namelist > sorted ; cat sorted ; rm sorted)&

will now execute these commands in background mode.

Stopping background commands

When a command is activated to execute in the background, the shell displays a number, called the *process number*, which identifies that particular command. It is important to make a note of this number, because the only way you can stop that command from going on (should you decide to cancel it for whatever reason), is to type

$ kill process__number

Using the command **kill** is the only way you can terminate the specified background process. Typing any other key or key sequence (like Ctrl D), has no effect.

SHELL PROCEDURES

Apart from the ability to execute commands, in either immediate or background mode, known collectively as *command line* entry mode, the shell can read and execute commands contained in a file. Such a collection of commands in a file, known as *shell procedure* or *shell script*, is a program that can be used alone or as part of another program written in any other language, such as C or Fortran.

A number of UNIX commands are in reality shell procedures. Thus, having the ability to write your own shell procedure adds to the flexibility with which you can use and control the system. Furthermore, since shell procedures are ordinary text files, they are easy to write and maintain. To create a shell procedure you only need to collect together the commands which will accomplish a given task and then create a text file (using **ed** or any other screen editor) to contain them. Shell procedures can contain any system or shell commands.

As an example, we will create a shell procedure which lists the files in our 'home' directory, sorted by modification time. We could achieve this, of course, by simply typing

```
$ ls -t
```

at the command line prompt, but then this is only meant to be a very simple illustration on how to write a shell procedure, before embarking on more complex examples. Thus, first evoke the **ed** line editor, and then add the lines shown below.

```
$ ed
a
ls -t
.
w lsmod
q
$ chmod u + x lsmod
$ __
```

We choose to call the file **lsmod** (that is **ls** by time of **mod**ification). We then used the **chmod** command to give execution (**x**) permission to the file.

27

From now on, every time the **lsmod** name is typed at the prompt, the procedure is executed (provided it has been given execution permission) and the commands contained therein are obeyed, resulting in the required listing.

Shell variables

Shell variables names, consisting of letters, digits and the underscore character, can be used in the same way as in other programming languages. To such variable names, the user can assign values and from then on the value of each variable can be substituted into a command line or shell procedure by preceding its name by the $ sign. For example, we could assign to the variable name **message** a value, by typing

$ message = 'Your wish is my command'
or
$ show = 'ls -l documents'

From then on, we could use the variable names **message** or **show** in the same way as we would use their values. Thus, typing

$ echo $message
would result in the string

Your wish is my command

to be displayed on the screen, while typing

$ $show

would list the files in the sub-directory **documents** in 'long' format.

If further characters follow a variable name, then the variable name must be enclosed in braces ({ }) which acts as delimiters. For example, typing

$ ${ message } s

would display the string "Your wish is my commands". Had we left out the braces, the result would have been a blank, as no value had been assigned to variable **messages**.

Some variable names have a special meaning to the shell. For example,

$PATH

is a list of directories which are searched when the shell attempts to execute a command. If **PATH** is not set, then the currently logged directory is searched by default.

When the shell is ready to accept input at the command line, it issues a $ prompt. This default prompt can be changed by the user by assigning a value to the shell's special variable **PS1**, which stands for 'primary prompt string'. Similarly, the 'secondary prompt string' **PS2**, which is displayed if the shell requires more input from the user, can also be changed from its default value (which is >) to another value.

To find out the state of these special shell variables, use the set command, as follows:

$ set

which invokes the response

HOME = /u/user1
IFS =

PATH = /bin:/usr/bin:/etc:/u/bin:/u/user1/bin::
PS1 = $
PS2 = >
SHELL = /bin/sh
TERM = ibm3161
$

where variable **IFS** stands for 'internal field separators' and shows the characters that the shell accepts as filed separators with the default values set to 'blank', 'tab' and 'new line'. The variable **TERM** shows what type of terminal is in use. Such information is needed by commands or programs for their proper functioning.

These and other variable names special to the shell, some of which are given default values by the shell, while some have to be set by the user, but all can be reset, are listed below. For a complete list see your local operating system reference manual.

CDPATH	the variable that informs shell where to search for the argument to a cd command, whenever that argument is not a 'null' and does not begin with '/' , '.' or ' .. '
HOME	the name of your login directory
MAIL	the path name of the file where your mail is placed
PATH	the list of directories searched by a given command
PS1	the variable that specifies the primary prompt string
PS2	the variable that specifies the secondary prompt string
!	the process number of the last process run in background
#	the number of positional parameters
$	the process number of the current shell
—	the current shell qualifiers
?	the exit status of the last command run. Zero indicates that command was completed successfully, non-zero indicates otherwise

Command substitution
When a shell command is required as part of the string assignment to a variable, then the command must be enclosed in reverse apostrophes and the whole string, including the command, in double quotes. For example,

$ where = "You are in `pwd`"
$ echo $where

will produce the response

30

You are in u/user1

Had the command **pwd** not been enclosed with in reverse apostrophes, the shell would have not been able to substitute the standard output of **pwd**, but would have taken it literally as part of the rest of the string. Similarly, had we enclosed the assignment string with single quotes, the command **pwd** would have been taken literally, whether it had been enclosed in reverse apostrophes or not. However, **where** always displays the directory in which the **where** assignment was originally made.

The read command

Just like the reverse apostrophe in command substitution, the **read** command allows the indirect assignment of values to variables by taking a line from the standard input device (usually the keyboard) and assigning each string from that line (one at a time) to named variables. For example, the command

read A B C

will await for input from the keyboard, and if we type

first second third

the **read** command produces the same result as if the assignment statement

A = first B = second C = third

had been made. Note that multiple assignments can be made in one line, provided they are separated by a space.

Positional parameters

The shell accepts a second type of variable, called 'positional parameter' which causes a shell procedure to refer to the command line for its value. The positional parameter **$0** refers to the first string on the command line (usually the name of the command), while $1 up to $9 refer to the second, and up to the tenth, string on the command line. For example, the following procedure would always display the third string typed in the command line (that is, the value of the positional parameter $2), every time the command and its arguments are entered.

31

```
$ ed
a
echo $2
.
w midpig
q
$ chmod u + x midpig
$
-
```

Now, every time the procedure **midpig** is evoked and three arguments are given, the middle argument is echoed on the screen. For example,

$ midpig Alan Bob Clive

will display

Bob

as the pig in the middle. Each time you run this procedure you can use different arguments.

The special parameter **$*** can be used to substitute all the supplied arguments, except for **$0** (the name of the command). For example, a file containing

cat $*

will display the contents of all the supplied filenames. A further advantage of using **$***, rather than the individual parameters (**$1**, **$2**, etc), is that more than 9 arguments can be supplied to a given command.

As well as being able to provide strings to the positional parameters of a shell procedure, we can find out how many arguments were given when the procedure was run, through the special parameter **$#**. For example, had we included

$ echo $#

as the last line in **midpig** and then run the procedure with three arguments, the shell would have responded with 3, being the number of arguments entered following the name of the procedure.

Later on, after we have considered shell control commands, we will be in a better position to write more advanced examples of shell procedures incorporating positional parameters.

SHELL CONTROL COMMANDS

Often, we may require a shell procedure to loop through its arguments, executing commands conditionally; doing one thing under certain conditions and another under different conditions. For example, we may require certain commands to be executed if the procedure receives a 'yes' as input, and certain other commands if the procedure receives a 'no'.

The shell provides control of flow with the following statements:

if	—structured conditional branching
case	—multiway branching
for	—looping over a list of commands
while	—conditional looping

These statements can be used either from within a shell procedure or by typing them at the command line, in which case the prompt will change to **$PS2** after the first line has been typed in and the Return key has been pressed.

The if..then..fi statement

The **if..then..fi** statement allows conditional branching which means that we can decide whether to execute certain commands or not. The decision depends on the outcome of the last executed command in the command-list which follows the if statement. If a zero status (true) is returned, the command-list following the then is executed, otherwise the statement is ended with **fi** which marks the end of the conditional branching. In general we can think of the statement as follows:

```
if command-list__1
   then command-list__2
fi
```

The exit status (return code) of the last executed command in the command-list1, following the **if** statement, can be found with the use of the **test** command which was specially written for use within a shell procedure. The test command takes the form:

test [qualifiers] filename

with the most commonly used qualifiers being:

33

− d	true if file is a directory
− f	true if file exists
− r	true if file can be read
− s	true if file exists and is not empty
− w	true if file can be written to

Another form of the command is:

test string

which returns true status if 'string' is not a null.

To illustrate the use of the **test** command, consider the following procedure.

```
if test -d $*
    then echo $* is a directory
fi
```

which we create using the **ed** line editor and name **whatis**. Don't forget to give the procedure execute permission. From then on, we can call the procedure and give it an argument, as follows:

$ whatis documents

which, if **documents** is indeed a directory would invoke the response

documents is a directory

otherwise nothing will be displayed but the prompt.

The if..then..else..fi statement
In many cases we might want to execute different commands if the last command to be executed in command-list__1, following the if statement, returns a non-zero (false) value. In such a case the statement takes the following general form:

```
if command-list__1
    then command-list__2
    else command-list__3
fi
```

An example of this is included in the modified **whatis** procedure shown below.

```
if test − d $*
   then echo $* is a directory
   else echo $* is a file
fi
```

If the argument typed in after the procedure name is a directory,
then the command following **then** is executed, otherwise the
command following **else** is executed.

The case statement
The **case** statement is one of shell's aids to writing readable
procedures and provides an efficient alternative to multiple if
statements. For example, assume we had the code

```
day = $1
if test $day = S
     then echo Weekend
     else if test $day = M
           then echo Week day
           else if test $day = T
                then echo Week day
                else if test $day = W
                     then echo Week day
                     else if test $day = F
                          then echo Week day
                          fi
                     fi
                fi
           fi
     fi
```

where the = characters stand for the relational operator 'equal
to'. Another is ! = and stands for 'not equal to'.
   A more efficient way of writing this code would be with the
adoption of the **case** command, the general format of which is:

```
case string in
   pattern) command-list__1;;
   pattern) command-list__2;;
   —

   —

   —

   pattern) command-list__N;;
esac
```

The shell attempts to match 'string' with each pattern in turn. When a pattern that matches 'string' is found, the appropriate command-list is executed and the case command is terminated (because of the inclusion of **;;** - the double semicolon) with program control being past to **esac**, the end of the procedure, which is **case** spelled backwards.

Thus, adopting the **case** command in our previous example, we can write

```
day = $1
case $day in
  S) echo Weekend;;
  M) echo Week day;;
  T) echo Week day;;
  W) echo Week day;;
  F) echo Week day;;
esac
```

Typing the first letter (in upper case) of a named day, displays whether that day is part of the weekend or a week day. Any other character causes the program to display a null value.

The for loop
The **for** statement marks the beginning code which will be executed repeatedly according to the conditions supplied by the *control* variable within the **for** loop. The general form of the statement is

```
for variable [in word-list]
do
    command-list
done
```

with the [in word-list] portion of the statement being optional. The word-list is a series of strings separated by blanks. The shell executes commands in the command-list once for each word in the word-list, with **variable** taking each word in the word-list in turn as its value. Execution ends when there are no more words in the word-list.

When the optional part of the statement is omitted, then writing

for A

is equivalent to writing

for A in $*

which allows execution of the loop for each positional parameter (that is, each supplied argument), without having to predefine their number.

The following example will help to illustrate the use of the **for** loop.

```
for A in hour day week month year
do
  wc -c $A
done
```

On running this procedure, variable A is first assigned to the word 'hour' and then the **wc** command (which stands for word count) is executed with the specified qualifier which causes the number of characters in variable A to be returned. The process is repeated with variable A taking in turn the values 'day', 'week', 'month' and 'year'. The looping ends when no more words (arguments) are available.

The while and until loops

The **while** loop provides a mechanism for repeating a list of commands. The general form of the statement is:

```
while command-list__1
do
  command-list__2
done
```

The shell executes command-list__1 and if successful, it executes command-list__2. This is repeated while execution of command-list__1 is successful, otherwise looping ends.

The **until** command causes the shell to execute a loop until execution of command-list__1 is not successful. Its general format is:

```
until command-list__1
do
  command-list__2
done
```

Thus, the **while** and the until loops test for opposite conditions. When these conditions fail, the loop ends.

The break and continue commands
There are two shell commands which cause unconditional program branching. These are: the **break** and the **continue** commands. The **break** ends a **while**, an **until** and a **for** loop, while the **continue** causes the immediate execution of the next iteration of a loop and, as such, alters the flow of control within a loop.

Of these two commands, the use of the **continue** command should be severely restricted, as it is possible to write code to carry out the same program flow in more efficient way, while the **break** command should only be used with the **case** command.

The exit command
The shell also allows one procedure to execute another, in which case it is desirable for the calling procedure to check the status of commands from the executing procedure; it provides a method of terminating a process before the process reaches an EOF (end-of-file).

If the **exit** command has an argument, it sets the status of process to the value of that argument. Thus, **exit 0** in a procedure causes the exit status of that procedure to be **0** (that is, successful), while omitting the argument from **exit**, causes it to return the status of the last executed command. These returned values can then be examined by the calling procedure to check whether the process has been completed successfully before continuing with its own processing.

The shift command
The **shift** command is used with positional parameters to shift to the left one argument at a time. For example, if we executed a command with positional parameters **$1**, **$2** and **$3** and then used the shift command, the very next time the command with the positional parameters was used, **$1** would have been discarded, **$2** would have taken the place of **$1** and **$3** the place of **$2**.

The following procedure will help to demonstrate the use of the shift command. Use the **ed** line editor to enter the commands shown below, and then use the **chmod** command to give the procedure execution permission.

```
while test $# != 0
do
  echo $*
  shift
done
```

Now execute the program giving it the arguments A, B, C, D and E. What appears on the screen is:

```
ABCDE
BCDE
CDE
DE
E
```

Spend a few seconds working out how the **shift** command is responsible for the displayed output.

* * *

The shell has many more commands which can be used to control your UNIX environment in special ways. However, this is an area which lies beyond the scope of this book. What is covered in this guide is more than enough to allow the user effective control of their environment. It is strongly suggested that you spend some time practising with the various commands presented and that you actually write your own procedures. Once you have done this, then the more advanced features of the shell could be explored.

* * *

COMMAND SUMMARY

The following is a summary of the most useful commands, from the user's point of view, supported by the UNIX operating environment. For a full list of both commands and qualifiers, consult your system's documentation.

Command

Explanation

alias

assigns an alias for commands, files or devices. Only available in the csh shell.

Example: $ alias t time

Allows t to be used in place of time.

cat [qualifiers]

Concatenates (joins) a file or files and lists the result.

Qualifiers:
—n No. of lines starting from 1
—s eliminates consecutive blank lines

Example: $ cat file1 file2

cd [directory]

Changes logged directory.

Example: $ cd /u/user1/docs

chmod [mode]

Changes permissions to files of directories.

Mode: [ugoa] [+-=] [rwxstugo]

where the optional characters within the various square brackets have the following meaning:

[ugoa]

u	user (owner)
g	group
o	others
a	all

41

	[+ - =]		
	+	add permissions
	–	subtract permissions
	=	replace permissions

[rwxstugo]

	r	read
	w	write
	x	execute
	s	set owner or group identity
	t	save text
	ugo	user/group/others— permission to be taken from present mode

Example: $ chmod go + r prog1.for

Adds read permission to members of the group and others.

cmp	Compares two files and prints the line number and character where they differ.

Example: $ cmp file1 file2

comm [qualifiers]	Compares two files for common lines.

Qualifiers:
—1 suppresses lines only in file1
—2 suppresses lines only in file2
—3 suppresses lines in both files

Example: $ comm – 12 file1 file2

Lists lines only common to both.

cp [qualifier]	Copies file1 (source) to file2 (destination).

Qualifier:
—i interactively protects destination file, if it already exists, from being overwritten

Example: $ cp -i file1 file2

42

date	Displays date on the screen.
diff [qualifiers]	Lists difference in two files or directories.
	Qualifiers: —b ignores trailing blanks —e prints ed changes required to make files identical
	Example $ diff -b file1 file2
ed	Accesses the **ed** line editor.
find [qualifiers]	Finds and lists a file or files.
	Qualifiers: —atime n where n is number of days since last access —links n with n number of links —mtime n where n is number of days since last modification —name filename —newer most recently modified
	Example: $ find —atime 3 —print
	Lists all files (—print must be included) not accessed during the last 3 days.
grep [qualifiers]	Searches a file for a pattern.
	Qualifiers: —c prints the count of matches —n lists line number with match
	Example: $ grep —n Hello filename
head	Prints first 10 lines in a file. (**tail** in the AIX version of UNIX)
jobs [qualifier]	Lists the background jobs.
	Qualifier: —1 displays process identity
	Example: $ jobs —1

kill	Terminate background job.
	Example $ kill job__number
ls [qualifiers]	Lists files in logged directory in alphabetical order.
	Qualifiers: —a all files —c in order of creation —g give group identity —l in long format —s in block size —t sorted by modification time —u sorted on last access time
	Example: $ ls -acl
mail	Receives and sends mail.
	Examples: Receive: $ mail
	Send: $ mail login__name(s) $ message $ Ctrl d
mkdir	Makes (creates) a directory.
	Example: $ mkdir docs
more	Lists contents of files a page at a time (**pg** in AIX version of UNIX)
	Example: $ more longfile
mv [qualifier]	Moves file1 (source) to file2 (destination) which renames a file.
	Qualifier: —i interactively protects destination file, if it already exists, from being overwritten
	Example: mv —i file1 file2

44

passwd	Changes password.
pg	Lists contents of files a page at a time. (Available in AIX version of UNIX - on other versions, use **more**)
pr [qualifiers]	Prints a file.
	Qualifiers: —ln where n is the page length (default is 66 lines) —wn where n is the page width (default 72 characters)
pwd	Prints working directory.
rm [qualifiers]	Removes files from directories.
	Qualifiers: —i interactively protects existing files —r recursively removes directory files
	Examples: $ rm file1 $ rm docs/file1
rmdir	Removes directory if empty.
sort [qualifiers]	Sorts or merges files.
	Qualifiers: —b ignores blanks —d dictionary order —f fold upper to lower case —i ignores characters outside the printable ASCII set —n sorts numbers by value —o directs output to a file —r sorts in reverse order
	Example: $ sort —nr file.dta
spell	Checks spelling within a file.
tail n	Lists last n lines of a file, if n is negative, or starts listing on nth line, if n is positive.

time	Displays the execution time of a command.
unalias	Removes a previous alias. Only applicable in **csh** shell.
vi	Accesses **vi** screen editor.
wc [qualifiers]	Counts number of lines, words and characters in a file.

Qualifiers:
—c counts only characters
—l counts only lines
—w counts only words

INDEX